HOW TO DEVELOP AND WRITE A RESEARCH PAPER

PHYLLIS CASH

Herbert H. Lehman College

Prentice Hall
New York • London • Toronto • Sydney • Tokyo • Singapore

94 18298

Prentice Hall General Reference
15 Columbus Circle
New York, NY 10023

An Arco Book

Arco, Prentice Hall, and colophons are
registered trademarks of Simon & Schuster, Inc.

Library of Congress Cataloging-in-Publication Division

Cash, Phyllis.
  How to develop and write a research paper / by Phyllis Cash—2nd ed.
  p. cm.
Bibliography: p.
ISBN 0-671-87939-1
1. Report writing. 2. Research. I. Title.
LB2369.C36   1988   88-14156
808'.02—dc19   CIP

Manufactured in the United States of America

7   8   9   10

CONTENTS

DEDICATION

This book is dedicated to the
most important men in my world:
Mark, Steve, David, and Sid.

ACKNOWLEDGMENTS

For permission to excerpt and reprint material in this book, the author and publisher are grateful to the following:

Lehman College
for the use of the library facilities and assistance of their librarians.

Simon and Schuster
for excerpts from *The Psychology of Achievement*, by Walter B. Pitkin. Copyright © 1930 by Walter B. Pitkin.

for excerpt from *After Conviction*, by Ronald L. Goldfarb and Linda R. Singer. Copyright © 1973 by Ronald L. Goldfarb and Linda R. Singer.

for excerpt from *Political Handbook & Atlas of the World, 1968*, by Walter H. Mallory, ed. Copyright © 1968 by The Council on Foreign Relations.

Salvatore L. Scorzello for the research paper "The Condition of the American Indians."

The H. W. Wilson Company
for material from the *Readers' Guide to Periodical Literature*. Reprinted by permission of the publisher, The H. W. Wilson Company.

Prentice-Hall, Inc.
for excerpt from *The Artist*, by Edmund Burke Feldman. Copyright © 1982 by Prentice-Hall, Inc.

INTRODUCTION

A term paper—often called a research paper—is a work that presents the results of the writer's investigation of a particular topic. Although an occasional research paper may be based wholly or partially on interviews and personal observation, the great majority of such investigations are carried out in a library, where the writer gathers facts and expert opinions from books, periodicals, and other sources.

Although the research paper is based on the ideas and work of others, you should not think of it as a mechanical process. In summarizing and relating facts and ideas from several sources, you will have the opportunity to use your creativity and show the kind of thinking of which you are capable. You will also, of course, be demonstrating your ability to express your ideas effectively and gracefully.

Over the years, a standard procedure for doing a research paper has evolved. This book is a step-by-step guide to this standard procedure. Both the procedure and this book are divided into three parts: the first part (Steps 2–5) is concerned with finding an appropriate subject; the second (Steps 6–10) deals with the research process; the third (Steps 11–16) gives help in writing the paper. When you have completed all of these steps, you will have a finished paper ready to hand in.

Most of the steps in this book are divided into two sections: Presentation and Application. The Presentation sections give information and principles that you will need to complete a particular step. Each of the Application sections gives detailed guidance in applying what you have learned to the term paper that you are writing, as you work through this book.

UNIT ONE
DEVELOPING THE SUBJECT

When instructors assign research papers, they usually mention a fairly broad subject within which students are expected to find their own topics. For example, an instructor in an American literature course might ask for a paper on any author studied in the course. A music teacher may require a paper on any phase of twentieth-century music. A history professor may ask students to investigate any aspect of the American labor movement. In each of these cases, it is the student's job to develop a specific topic that can be adequately treated in the length of paper that has been assigned.

The steps in this unit are concerned with how you go about selecting a specific subject, how you decide what organizational pattern will be most appropriate, and how you develop a thesis statement, that is, a brief statement of what you intend to do in your paper. These initial steps are designed to provide a focus for your research. Therefore, they should be completed before you go to the library.

At the same time, however, you should also look upon these early decisions as tentative. As you do research and get deeper into your subject, you are likely to look at things differently, and this may well lead to adjustments in your topic, in your chosen pattern of organization, or in your thesis statement. You should not regard such changes in course as setbacks. They are, rather, signs that you are doing some good thinking and are getting nearer to your goal.

Step 1—Getting Started

Each paper has basic requirements that you should take into account right from the beginning:

1. Date due: As assigned by your instructor. The recommended schedule for doing the steps in this book takes from seven to nine weeks (see the breakdown with the Contents of this book). This will allow you to proceed carefully and also give adequate time for any necessary reconsiderations or revisions.

2. Length: As assigned. A *page* usually means double-spaced typing on 8½-by-11-inch paper. Such a page contains about 250 words.

3. Footnotes: Every research paper must have a system for showing where the writer found the information he is using. Each discipline has its own specific form (see Step 13). In this book, we are going to use the forms most commonly used in the humanities. They are found in the Documentation section in Appendix B.

4. Bibliography or References: A listing of the sources you have used is placed at the end of the paper. As with footnotes, each discipline has its own form (see Step 14). To be consistent, the forms commonly used in the humanities are found in the Documentation section in Appendix B.

5. Cover sheet: You should provide an initial page that includes the title of the paper, the name or number of the course for which it was written, the instructor's name, your name, and the date.

Appendix D contains a detailed Self-Evaluation Guide, which you may use to check your completed paper. You will find it helpful to read it over now to get an idea of the standards that you will have to meet.

In addition to this book you will need the following to complete your paper:

1. Two sizes of ruled index cards, 3-by-5-inch for listing sources and 4-by-6-inch for taking notes.

2. A dictionary for checking spelling, syllabication, meaning, etc.

3. A thesaurus or book of synonyms for helping you use a variety of words in your writing.

4. A basic grammar book for checking correct grammatical forms.

[Note: if you are writing a paper in the social sciences or the natural sciences, you will need a formbook or handbook for subject-specific documentation. See Steps 13 and 14.]

Step 2—Choosing a Topic

Your first task is to take the assignment as given by your instructor and develop for yourself an appropriate topic. In order to do this it helps to know what the characteristics of a good topic are, as well as some of the main ways that a topic can be defective.

Presentation

A research paper is expected to be a detailed examination of a particular topic; it is also expected to be based on a variety of sources. A topic is too broad if a much longer paper than you are to write would be required to treat it in a detailed fashion. A topic is too narrow if a sufficient variety of sources cannot be found with which to work. Whether a topic is too narrow depends, therefore, to some extent on the resources of the library that you plan to use for your research. A topic is too personal if it relies heavily on your own feelings, experiences, and opinions. A topic is too technical if the research requires specialized knowledge that you are unable to provide.

In the table on page 4, there are some topics that have been developed from five different subjects. Study them and try to decide why they are labeled (1) too broad, (2) inappropriate, or (3) good to start with.

Application

Now you are ready to develop your own topic. There are several strategies that will help you discover a topic that is both suitable and interesting.

Objective: To choose a topic for the paper you have been asked to write.

Procedures: (See Appendix A)

1. Focused Free Writing: Keeping the area of assigned research in mind, write continuously for at least ten minutes. It is most important to keep writing; do not lift your pencil from your paper. Write down whatever comes into your head about the assignment. This may include questions and statements, in any order in which they occur to you. When the focused free-writing time is up, reread what you have written. Underline any statement or question that you would like to continue writing about. Do any

SAMPLE TOPICS

SUBJECT	TOO BROAD	INAPPROPRIATE	GOOD TO START WITH
20th-century music	popular music	why I like the Beatles (too personal)	imagery in the Beatles' songs
19th-century military history	the West and the Indians	my opinion of Sitting Bull (too personal)	Sitting Bull and Custer's Last Stand
the American labor movement	unionism in America	organizing a union local (too technical)	how the paraprofessionals working for the New York City Board of Education became part of the United Federation of Teachers
the history of ethnic groups in the United States	the history of the Puerto Ricans	one reason for Puerto Rican migration to the mainland (too narrow)	an analysis of Puerto Rican migration to the mainland in the 1940s
any author studied in your American literature course	Emerson as a famous American writer	Emerson as a child (too narrow)	Hindu philosophy and Emerson

of your sentences seem particularly interesting? Do any of them seem to cluster around one topic? Do you think you would like to find answers to any of your questions? Make a list of all of the topics you have developed through focused free writing. Now continue with 2 below.

2. Brainstorming: Take a good-size piece of paper (8½-by-11), and in the center write one word or a short phrase to represent the area of research you have been assigned. Then, for ten minutes, write down every word that comes to mind when you think of this area. When you have finished, carefully analyze your responses. Do any of them cluster together? Form columns of all words that seem to relate to each other. Do any of the columns suggest a suitable and interesting topic? Continue with 3 below.

3. Listing: List all of the topics you can think of that fall within the assigned area. Then go over your list, marking each topic with a B if it is too broad, an I if it is inappropriate, or a G if it would be a good starting topic. Now consider the topics marked G and decide which one you would like to work with. If you are not satisfied with the topics you have come up with, wait a day or two and repeat the procedures. Remember that you will be spending several weeks working on your topic, so you should try to choose something that really interests you.

Step 3—Matching the Topic with Organizational Patterns

Once you have decided on your topic, it is important to begin thinking about how you can develop it. One of the best ways to proceed is to consider different organizational patterns and decide which one or which ones would be appropriate for your topic.

Presentation

Here are the five most common organizational patterns:

1. Chronological: this pattern treats a topic according to its time sequence. *Example:* Using the topic *an analysis of Puerto Rican migration to the mainland in the 1940s,* you might concentrate on

the years 1940, 1943, 1946, and 1949. You could then point out and explain the trends in Puerto Rican migration that developed during the decade.

2. Comparison-Contrast: This pattern takes two or more aspects of a topic and shows how they are similar and how they differ. *Example:* Using the topic *Hindu philosophy and Emerson,* you might discuss the characteristics of Hindu philosophy and then show the ways in which Emerson's work is similar and the ways in which it is different.

3. Topical: This pattern breaks a topic into smaller units, or subtopics, and analyzes each one. *Example:* Using the topic *imagery in the Beatles' songs,* you might discuss and analyze the symbolism related to such subtopics as drugs and sexual mores.

4. Problem-Solution: This pattern states a problem and then analyzes the solutions proposed by experts in the field. The student may even develop his own solution if he can support it with the research he has done. *Example:* Using the topic *how the paraprofessionals working for the New York City Board of Education became part of the United Federation of Teachers,* you could discuss the problems the paraprofessionals faced as nonunion members, the problems involved in joining an established union, and the solutions found to these problems by the groups and experts involved.

5. Opinion-Reason: This pattern allows the student to state his opinion about his topic and show how the reasons for this opinion are well supported by the research he has done. *Example:* Using the topic *Sitting Bull and Custer's Last Stand,* you could express the opinion that a myth has developed that unjustifiably pictures Sitting Bull as a villain and Custer as a hero. Your reasons for this opinion would be shown by your analysis of the myths and historical information about this famous battle.

You may use one organizational pattern or a combination. In fact, it is common to find that two or more organizational patterns are naturally related to a topic. *Example:* Using the topic *an analysis of Puerto Rican migration to the mainland in the 1940s,* you could use a chronological pattern as suggested above. Then, within each time period, you could treat as subtopics (topical organization) the various factors that led to migration, such as economic, political, and social factors. Finally, you could give reasons for your opinion as to which of these factors was most important (opinion-reason).

Application

Now you are ready to choose organizational patterns for your own paper. Follow the procedure outlined below.

Objective: To choose patterns of organization that might be used in developing your topic.

Procedure:

1. Write down your topic from Step 2.

   _____

2. Write the patterns (one or a combination) that you could use for development.

   _____

3. In a few sentences combine 1 and 2 and show *how* you will use the patterns to develop your topic.

   _____
   _____
   _____

Step 4—Preparing an Idea Sheet

Application

At this point you have a starting topic and an idea of the patterns of organization you could use to develop it. You must explore this topic in more depth before you can begin your research. One way to do this is to prepare an idea sheet. The following procedure will show you how to do this.

Objective: To develop an idea sheet that will further refine your starting topic.

Procedure:

1. Do some general reading on your topic, keeping in mind which organizational patterns you have decided will be most promising. This preliminary survey should include the following: (a) a general encyclopedia article; and (b) any information you already have, such as class notes, textbooks, and other assigned readings.

2. Focused Free Writing: Use this technique once again. Now, however, make your topic the focus of your free writing.

3. Question Development: Using the question words—*who, what, where, when, why, how*—list all of the questions you think pertain to your topic. Do any of them seem to fit together as part of a major question your paper will try to answer?

4. List all ideas, questions, and reactions that come to mind during this preliminary survey. This idea sheet will help you later in structuring your research. While you are preparing it, you may find that your topic is changing and becoming more definite and limited. You may also see new possibilities for using different organizational patterns. You may even find you have so many ideas that you need several pages. All this is progress!

Step 5—Formulating a Thesis Statement

Once you have chosen a topic, thought about the organizational patterns you might use, and prepared an idea sheet, you are ready for the next important step—formulating a thesis statement. A thesis statement consists of one or two sentences that express what you plan to do with your topic; it is a statement of the aim, the goal, and the main idea of your paper. It should contain an idea that can be developed through scholarly research and that can serve as a tool for maintaining the unity of your paper. All sections of your paper and all of the research you use must be related to your thesis statement. As your work on the paper progresses, your topic, organizational patterns, and thesis statement should become closely intertwined. Together they will provide a firm basis for your research.

TOPIC	ORGANIZATIONAL PATTERNS	THESIS STATEMENT
imagery in the Beatles' songs	Topical—discuss the imagery involving sex and drugs and Chronological—use the earliest songs first	The lyrics of the Beatles' songs use a great deal of imagery. Much of this reflects the mores of our culture involving sex and drugs.
Sitting Bull and Custer's Last Stand	Comparison-contrast—show the difference between the myths and the historic realities of Custer's Last Stand	There is a discrepancy between the myth and the reality of Sitting Bull's participation in the battle called Custer's Last Stand. The myth falsely depicts Sitting Bull as a villain and Custer as a hero.
how the paraprofessionals working for the New York City Board of Education became part of the United Federation of Teachers	Problem-solution—show how this group solved the problems of joining an established union and Chronological—trace this movement historically from beginning to end	The paraprofessionals working for the New York City Board of Education are a recent example of workers who were able to join an established, recognized union.

TOPIC

an analysis of Puerto Rican migration to the mainland in the 1940s

Hindu philosophy and Emerson

ORGANIZATIONAL PATTERNS

Opinion-reason—identify the factors that led to this migration and explain how your research proves they were important

and

Topical—treat each of the factors under logical subtopics

and

Chronological—organize these factors in the order in which they developed historically

Topical—analyze the aspects of Hindu philosophy that appear in Emerson's writings

and

Comparison-contrast—show the similarities in Emerson's writings and Hindu literature

THESIS STATEMENT

The Puerto Rican migration to the mainland in the 1940s was caused by several factors.

Emerson, in his poetry and essays, shows the influence of Hindu philosophy and literature.

Presentation

In the table on pages 9–10, there are examples of good thesis statements based on the same topics and organizational patterns presented in Steps 2 and 3.

The preceding thesis statements are good because:

1. They consist of one or two complete sentences.

2. They state the definite topic of the paper.

3. They give an idea of the approach the writer will take.

4. They are closely related to the set of organizational patterns to be used.

5. They can be developed by using sources of expert information—in other words, by research.

Application

You are now ready to formulate your own thesis statement for the paper you are writing. Review quickly all of the work you have done for your paper so far and all that you have just learned about thesis statements. Then follow the procedure below.

Objective: To formulate a thesis statement for your paper on the basis of your topic, your patterns of organization, and your idea sheet.

Procedure:

1. Study and analyze your idea sheet. Group ideas that seem to be related. Are there any ideas that you find especially interesting?

2. Focused Free Writing: Now you can use the focused free-writing technique again. This time keep in mind the ideas that interest you and write, nonstop, for at least ten minutes. Read over what you have written and underline any sentences that could be developed into a thesis statement.

3. Questioning: Using your idea sheet and/or your focused free writing, list as many questions as you can think of. Analyze your question list. Do any of them seem related? Can you change these quesions into thesis statements?

4. Check your thesis statement to be sure that it includes both the topic and what you plan to do with the topic. Your thesis statement should also contain an idea that can be developed by research.

5. Be prepared to repeat 1, 2, and 3. Formulating a thesis statement is challenging, creative work and may take a great deal of trial and error before you are satisfied.

UNIT TWO
FINDING THE MATERIAL

The steps in Unit One were a preparation for research. In Unit Two the scene changes to the library. The steps in this unit will show you how to investigate the resources of your own library, how to find books and articles that are likely to contain useful material, and how to prepare bibliography cards and note cards. When you complete this unit, you should be ready to begin organizing your material and writing your paper.

Step 6—Exploring the Library

Application

To complete this step you must actually go to the library you plan to use for your research. Answering the questions below will be an efficient way for you to learn how to use it. Following the questions are suggested activities that involve actual use of the library.

Objective: To use questions and activities to learn how to use your library for research.

Procedure:

1. Go to the library and answer the following questions:

   a. Do you know where each of the following is located? Many libraries have maps posted that will help you.

      (1) card catalogs.

      (2) indexes for periodicals, newspapers, and scholarly journals.

      (3) volumes of abstracts.

      (4) different kinds of books: reference, reserve, circulating, special collections.

      (5) periodicals.

(6) audiovisual materials: tapes, cassettes, records, slides, filmstrips, microfilm, microfiche.

b. Do you know how to use the catalogs, indexes, and abstracts? Do you know where to find books on open shelves? Do you know the procedures for obtaining materials from closed stacks? Can you operate the audiovisual equipment? Have you explored the facilities for making copies? If your library has installed a computerized system for locating material, do you know how to use it?

2. If you answered no to any part of question 1, see the librarian at once for help.

3. Make a floor plan of your library.

4. (a) Find one card in the catalog for each of the following:

(1) subject card: Hopi Indians

(2) title card: A History of Art and Music

(3) author card: Oscar Lewis

(b) Make out a call slip for one card you found in activity (a) if you need one to get your book.

(c) List all of the information you can find on one of the cards you found in activity (a).

5. (a) Find one entry in the *Reader's Guide to Periodical Literature* for 1988 for each of the following:

(1) subject: AIDS

(2) author: Peter G. Davis

(b) Make out a call slip for one entry you found in activity (a) if you need one to get your periodical.

(c) List all of the information you can find in one of the entries you found in activity (a).

(d) Actually locate one of the articles in one of the entries you found in activity (a).

6. If any of these activities has given you trouble, see the librarian at once for help.

Step 7—Finding Appropriate Sources

Now you are ready to do independent research for your own topic and thesis. The school library is usually the best place to begin. When you go, be sure to take the following supplies with you:

1. Several pencils for writing bibliography cards and note cards.

2. A ballpoint pen for filling out call slips.

3. Bibliography cards—3-by-5-inch ruled index cards.

4. Note cards—4-by-6-inch ruled index cards (some students use even larger ones).

5. This book; you will especially need the Documentation section in Appendix B as a guide to preparing your cards.

When you get to the library, look up the subject of your paper in the card catalog and in the periodical indexes. If you have trouble finding your subject, ask the librarian for help. Sometimes the catalog system will use a synonym that doesn't occur to you. For example, one student started his research by looking up "family planning" and found nothing. When he asked the librarian, he learned that his subject was listed under "birth control."

Once you've found your subject, read through the catalog cards and index entries. If any book or article seems as if it might be worthwhile, follow the library's procedure for obtaining it.

Presentation

Below are three sets of topics and thesis statements, along with a catalog card and an index entry that seem appropriate for each one. Notice how several parts of the catalog card can be used to decide whether a book will be a good source.

1. Topic: Sitting Bull and Custer's Last Stand

   Thesis: There is a discrepancy between the myth and the reality of Sitting Bull's participation in the battle called Custer's Last Stand. The myth falsely depicts Sitting Bull as a villain and Custer as a hero.

E 83 .876 .C983 R67	**Rosenberg, Bruce A** Custer and the epic of defeat [by] Bruce A. Rosenberg. University Park, Pennsylvania State University Press [1974] 313 p. illus. 24 cm. Includes bibliographical references. ISBN 0-271-01172-6 1. Custer, George Armstrong, 1839–1876. 2. Heroes. 3. Legends—History and criticism. I. Title.

E83.876.C983R67   973.8'1'0924 [B]   74–14631
                                                          MARC
Library of Congress   75

Custer, George Armstrong. 1839–1876
                                    about

Ghosts on the Little Bighorn. R. P. Jordan. il por supp
   (folded map) map *Natl Geogr* 170:786–813 D '86

Post-mortem at the Little Bighorn. D. D. Scott and
   M. A. Connor. il maps *Nat Hist* 95:46–55 Je '86

Post-mortem of the post-mortem [discussion of June 1986
   article Post-mortem at the Little Bighorn] D. D. Scott
   and M. A. Connor. *Natl Hist* 95:2–3 Ag '86

Unearthing Little Bighorn's secrets, J. Robbins. il por
   map *Natl Parks* 60:16–23 N/D '86

2. Topic: Imagery in the Beatles' songs

> Thesis: The lyrics of the Beatles' songs use a great deal of imagery. Much of this imagery reflects the mores of our culture involving sex and drugs.

Fine Art
ML
421
.B4
035
1983
	O'Grady, Terence J.
	    The Beatles, a musical evolution / by Terence J.
	O'Grady. — Boston: Twayne,1983.
	    216 p. : ill. ; 23 cm. — (Twayne's music series)
	    Bibliography: p. 201–203.
	    Discography: p. 193–200.
	    Includes index.
	    ISBN O-8057-9453-0
	
	    1. Beatles. I. Title. II. Series.
	    20 JAN 84 8954774 VYLLac 82-21288

Beatles
  George Harrison [interview] A. DeCurtis. por *Roll Stone*
    p.47–8 + N 5–D 10 '87

> Glimpse the truth [Help!: Rubber soul. Revolver, Sgt.
> Pepper's Loney Hearts Club Band] il *High Fidel*
> 37:94–9 + N '87

  Paul McCartney [interview] A. DeCurtis, por *Roll Stone*
    p39–40 + N 5–D 10 '87

  When stereo isn't stereo [releasing early non-stereo Beatles
    albums on stereo compact discs] M. Riggs. il *High
    Fidel* 37:5 D '87

3. Topic: Hindu philosophy and Emerson

Thesis: Emerson, in his poetry and essays, shows the influence of Hindu philosophy and literature.

---

814   **Emerson, Ralph Waldo,** 1803–1882.
     Essays. First series. New York, Clarke, Given & Hooper
Fm 3ess4 ₍n.d.₎
ser. 1

     iv, 326 p. (University edition)

     Binder's title: Emerson's essays, vol. I.

     Contents. — History. Self-reliance. Compensation. Spiritual laws. Love. Friendship. Prudence. Heroism. The over-soul. Circles. Intellect. Art.

Emerson, Kendall
Ray of hope in Russia. *Outlook* 124:74–6 Ja

 14 '20

Emerson, Ralph Waldo

> Belaboring the Brahmans again. *Lit Digest*
> 63:31 O 4 '19

Carlyle and Emerson. J. M. Sloan. *Liv Age*
 309:486–9 My 21 '21

Idol of compensation. M. Moravsky. *Nation*
 108:1004–5 Je 28 '19; Same cond. Our Opinion
 67:179–80 S '19

Application

Now you are ready to go to your library to research the topic and thesis of the paper you are writing.

Objective: To find as many sources of information as are required for your paper. Be sure to use both books and periodicals.

Procedure:

1. Using your topic and thesis statement, find books in the card catalog and articles in the indexes that seem appropriate for your paper.

2. Follow your library's procedures for using these materials.

3. You may find at this stage that you must revise or change your topic or thesis because there is too little or too much material. You may also find another, more exciting topic as you are working. Don't hesitate to modify your topic or your thesis; you still have enough time to complete your paper, and very little you have done so far will be wasted.

Step 8—Preparing Bibliography Cards

At this point in your research efforts, you have found materials that seem promising. Before you go on to examine these materials to see what kind of information they provide, you need to know how to make bibliography cards and note cards. The actual preparation of the bibliography—Step 14—is quite a way off. But you must begin now to handle your sources efficiently if you are to be ready for Step 14.

The bibliography is an alphabetical list of the sources from which you have taken information that you have used in your paper. Each entry in a bibliography must contain certain facts about the source, and these facts must be presented in an acceptable format. Experience has shown that the easiest way to do this is to prepare a bibliography card at the outset for each source from which information is taken. The bibliography card should contain all of the information that will later be needed in preparing both the bibliography and the footnotes. Should it happen that a source isn't used in the final paper, the card can always be discarded. On the other hand, incomplete or missing bibliography cards can only cause confusion and last-minute rushes to the library.

Sample bibliography cards for the two most common research sources—books and periodicals—are given in the Presentation below. Samples for other kinds of sources can be found in Appendix B.

Presentation

The following information must be included in the bibliography card for a book:

1. author's name, last name first.

2. title of the book, underlined.

3. where the book was published.

4. the publisher's name.

5. the year the book was published.

This information is usually found on the title page or on the copyright page. It should be arranged on a 3-by-5-inch card like this:

author's name	*Cash, Phyllis*
title	<u>How to Develop and Write a Research Paper</u>
where published	*New York*
publisher	*Arco*
year published	*1988*

The following information must be included in the bibliography card for a periodical:

1. author's name (of the article itself), last name first.

2. title of the article, in quotes.

3. name of the periodical, underlined.

4. volume number.

5. date of the periodical.

6. exact pages on which the article appears.

This information is usually found on the cover or the masthead page. It should be arranged on a 3-by-5-inch card as follows:

author's name	*Jones, Bill*
title of article	*"The Beatles Are Coming"*
title of periodical	*Modern Music*
volume number	*50*
date of periodical	*June 20, 1985*
exact pages of article	*pgs. 5 to 7 and 25 to 30*

Application

This Application should take place at the same time as the Application for Step 10, in which you will be examining the sources you have selected for information that is useful for your paper.

Objective: To write as many bibliography cards as are necessary for the paper you are writing.

Procedure:

1. Each time you find a source you think you may have a use for in your paper, make out a bibliography card.

2. Check to be sure you have included all of the information you will need, as shown in Appendix B.

Step 9—Preparing Note Cards

As you do your research you will need an efficient system for recording the information you find and for keeping track of where it came from. The bibliography card, which was described in Step 8, is one component of such a system; a second component is the note card.

A note card is simply a ruled index card, usually 4 by 6 inches but sometimes larger, that a researcher uses to record a piece of information that he thinks he may want to use. Such notes can take several forms: (1) a direct quote is a note that you have copied word for word from the source; (2) a paraphrase is a note in which you express another person's ideas in your own words; (3) in an outline note, you organize the material in terms of main and subordinate ideas; (4) the summary note is, like the paraphrase, written in your own words, but it is usually longer and covers much more source material. Note cards can also be used for copies of tables, charts, maps, graphs, etc.

Each note card must also include an indication of the source of the material it contains. Usually the author's last name is put at the top center of the card and the page number where the material was found is written in the upper right-hand corner. If you are using two books by the same author, or if the author of a source is not given, you can use part of the title to show where the material came from. It is not necessary to give more complete information about the source because you have already entered that information on a bibliography card. In most cases, you will have several note cards from a particular source but only one bibliography card.

In the upper left-hand corner of each note card, you should indicate in one or two words the aspect of your topic, or the subtopic, that the material on the card is related to. For example, if you are writing a paper on the history of baseball, you might have subtopics on your cards like "origin," "development," "present form." These subtopics will be very hepful when you organize your material and outline your paper.

Presentation

Following are examples of four different kinds of note cards. Preceding each card is the source material upon which it is based. Notice on each card the subtopic in the upper left-hand corner, the author or title in the center, and the page reference in the upper right-hand corner.

1. Direct Quote Note Card

---

244   THE PSYCHOLOGY OF ACHIEVEMENT

prodigiously into a ripe old age, never snapping back at the curs that were always yapping at his heels, never uttering an unkind word about foe or rival and never doing an unkind deed. But no more of this. The list is endless. Let him who would scan it further turn to the biographies of the great.

The Will to Get Well

The will to live amounts to little unless it is supported by the will to get well. Every physician knows that his hopeless cases are those in which the patient has lost interest in recovering. And his most amazing cures are usually worked upon people who burn with the desire to bounce to their feet

---

mental factors

244

Pitkin

"The will to live amounts to little unless it is supported by the will to get well. Every physician knows that his hopeless cases are those in which the patient has lost interest in recovering."

2. Paraphrase Note Card

ENERGY   223

accidents, personal misfortunes and similar causes strike down some superior men early in life. Eliminate these from the reckoning and the connection between high ability and animal energy stands forth.

Among many marks of health, two stand out as the surest and most deeply significant. They are a quick return to equilibrium after a shock and, secondly, high immunity. Both can be noted on the mental levels as well as on the grosser physical planes. And later we shall consider some interesting aspects and specimens. Be it noted in passing that in the intellectual life one of the manifestations of stable equilibrium is swift recovery from harsh criticism, personal rebuffs, financial failure, unpopularity, and similar misfortunes in which one's chosen work is involved. No man of superior ability in writing, in music, in politics, or in science is long withheld from

---

mental factors   223

Pitkin

Two aspects of good health are an ability to bounce back after trauma and a high resistance to such trauma (mental and physical).

3. Outline Note Card

PROBATION AN ALTERNATIVE TO PRISON   /   209

Since the police were paid seventy-five cents for every offender put in jail, they lost money every time Augustus succeeded in having someone released to his custody.

Augustus provided the seeds from which our system of probation has grown. Probation was first formally established in the United States. The system, since emulated by other countries, is considered America's contribution to progressive penology. Today over one half of all convicted offenders in the United States are placed on probation. In 1965 approximately 459,140 adults and 224,948 juveniles were on probation, while 475,042 adults and 123,256 juveniles were in institutions or on parole.[2] Under probation, sentences are suspended and defendants continue to live in their communities under conditions imposed by the court and supervised by probation officers.

Augustus provided probation with its characteristic feature: the personal services of a probation officer (a title that was not applied to Augustus himself but was used by his successors) who views his work with offenders as assistance rather than punishment. He was building, how-

---

Probation in U.S.   Goldfarb   .209

I.   ½ of all convicted offenders on probation

A.   1965:   459,140 adults
             224,948 juveniles } on probation

B.   1965:   475,042 adults
             123,256 juveniles } on probation

4. Summary Note Card

To be sure, advertising artists have something to sell, but they cannot sell it until they find out how the product is used. Hence, there is an emphasis on research into the social and psychological character of particular markets. That research might be undertaken for crassly commercial reasons; nevertheless, it introduces vital new elements to art.

First is the necessity of understanding a product thoroughly. The same requirement applies to the practice of industrial design: a purely optical understanding· of a product turns out to be inadequate for explaining its value or purpose, much less for changing its appearance.

Second is the necessity of understanding viewers—as members of a class, as people with special needs, as persons who think and act in certain ways. Again, Leonardo was first: he maintained that painters must understand the emotions of the witnesses to an accident if they wished to depict the event naturally and truthfully. To Leonardo that meant watching real people at real accidents. Direct observation, empirical research! For the graphic designer, inquiry lies at the foundation of artistic creativity.

Third is the serious study of human perception. The academic tradition, which remains alive in many places, simply overlooked the problem. If time and space are frozen, if nothing but the transmission of light energy takes place between objects and spectators, then artists cannot account for the· emotional and cognitive impact of images on viewers. The Renaissance artist, operating on the assumption of a fixed and unchangeable universe, needed no theory of perception beyond what could be derived from geometry and optics. Of course, that was a great deal, since it produced the science of perspective! But graphic designers are obliged to accomplish their objectives within a time frame as short as six seconds. So they need a deeper and more sophisticated theory of perception.

Visual memory, the duration of sensory excitation, the connections between optical and tactile feelings, the processes of symbol formation, age, sexual and educational influences on vision, subliminal perception, the stimulation of latent imagery, the interactions among media—all these factors impinge on the work of graphic designers. They are both the tools and the objects of research conducted by specialists in graphic information. Let us call them artists!

Fifty years ago illustrators would have been thrilled to exhibit in an art gallery, to see their work in museums. Today their successors in graphic design work at the cutting edge of visual art. The best designers are the shock troops of art's *avant garde.* And the gallery painters and printmakers know it.

Sources of
contemporary
art

Feldman   59

Advertising artists undertake research primarily for commercial reasons. This research includes understanding the product, understanding the viewers and studying the theories of human perception.

Sources of contemporary art (2)

60

Feldman

Other factors such as visual memory, sensory and optical experience, symbol formation, and interaction among media influence the graphic designer's work. All of this introduces vital new elements in Contemporary art.

Application

As with the Application for Step 8, this Application should take place at the same time as the Application for Step 10.

Objective: To write as many note cards as you will need for the paper you are writing.

Procedure:

1. Each time you come across information that you think will be useful, prepare a note card. Be sure to use the most appropriate note-taking skill (direct quote, paraphrase, outline, summary). You should use combinations of these skills whenever necessary.

2. Check to be sure you have included the subtopic, the author or title, and the page where you found the information.

Step 10—Finding Appropriate Information

Application

Now that you've found books and periodicals you think you can use, and now that you know how to prepare bibliography cards and note cards, you are ready to begin examining sources to see if you can locate and extract information that will be useful for your paper. In doing this, follow this procedure of previewing, skimming, and reading.

Objective: To use several sources to find appropriate information for your paper.

Procedure:

1. To find appropriate information in a book:

   (a) Look in the table of contents for relevant chapters.

   (b) Look in the index for pages that may contain relevant material.

   (c) Do the appendixes contain information you can use?

   (d) Is there a list of charts, maps, illustrations that may be helpful?

   (e) Once you've located the parts of the book that you can use, follow the suggestions under 2.

2. To find appropriate information in periodical articles:

   (a) Read the title, subtitles, and captions of illustrations within the selection.

   (b) Read the entire first paragraph of the selection.

   (c) Read the first line of every paragraph in the selection.

   (d) Read the entire last paragraph of the selection.

   (e) Do the charts, maps, or illustrations contain information you can use?

   (f) At any point where you think you've found something worthwhile, *read* that entire section carefully.

3. To take the information from the source:

   (a) When you've decided to use the book or article, immediately make out a bibliography card. (See Step 8.)

   (b) Make out a note card whenever you find information you think you can use. (See Step 9.)

4. Remember that any additional sources that you find in the books or articles you read should be investigated. Any bibliographies you find in these books and articles can lead you to more information.

5. Now that you are at the heart of the research process, you may find information that will lead you to change your topic or thesis. Be open-minded and ready to follow any intellectual trail that seems promising. Such an attitude will lead to a better paper.

UNIT THREE
WRITING THE PAPER

Now that you have collected all of your information, you must begin to think about organizing it and putting it in written form. The steps in this unit deal with outlining, with the problems of writing several drafts, with documentation through footnotes and a bibliography, and with typing and proofreading the final version. By the end of this unit you will have a completed paper ready to hand to your instructor.

Step 11—Outlining the Paper

The first step in actually writing your paper is to organize your information and ideas. The best way to do this is to make a detailed sentence outline of the entire paper. An outline can be revised easily and serves as the skeleton for your paper. If the outline is done well, the actual writing of the paper becomes much easier.

Before you start the outline, take all of your note cards and group them according to the subtopics you have put in the upper left-hand corner. Then arrange the cards in the order you think you will use them, rearranging them until they are as well organized as possible. Your note cards enable you to organize your paper by shuffling cards rather than by writing, rewriting, and crossing out.

When your cards have been arranged to your satisfaction, check to see that your topic, thesis, and note cards are unified. If they aren't, don't be afraid to change your topic or thesis to conform with the research you have done. You may also discover a need for additional research. If you have followed the suggested schedule, you still have three weeks in which to complete your work.

Once your note cards are organized, your subtopics become the main ideas in your outline, and your note cards can be used as supporting details and subdetails. As you do your outline, keep your note cards in the order in which they appear in the outline. After you've completed the outline, number your note cards consecutively and place the number of each note card next to the place you will use it in your outline. The outline will take a great deal of time. You may have to revise it many times. However, the better your outline, the easier it will be to write your paper.

Presentation

Outline A is a general form; Outline B is by a student.

Outline A

Your name   Course
Date   Instructor

Title of Your Paper

Thesis: Write your thesis statement here.
Pattern: List the patterns you will use here.

Paragraph
1.
{ Introduction:
    Write your opening sentences here. Be sure to include your thesis statement.

Development:

  I. Main Idea Sentence

    A. Supporting detail sentence

        1. subdetail sentence (if needed; use 2, 3, etc., if needed)

    B. Supporting detail sentence
    C. Supporting detail sentence (use D, E, F, etc., if needed)

 II. Another Main Idea Sentence

    A. Supporting detail sentence (if needed, use supporting details and subdetails as shown above)

III. Continue with as many paragraphs as you need for all of your main ideas.

Paragraphs
2., 3., 4., etc.

Final
paragraph

{

Conclusion:
  Summarize your paper; review the thesis statement; give your conclusions.

Outline B

David Shaffer   History 178
March 20, 1989   Dr. Sydney Gulker

More Could Have Been Done—Government,
Unions, and Black Employment

Thesis: During the 40s, 50s, and 60s the federal government and
some large trade unions were not as effective as was possible
in ending job discrimination against Black Americans.

Patterns: (a) Topical; (b) Comparison-Contrast

Introduction:

Black Americans have suffered many injustices as a minority group in
this country. One of the most devastating areas of racial injustice
concerns the economic aspects of the Black American's life. Much of
this injustice has been perpetuated by the federal government and some
large trade unions.

I. The federal government has been a passive agent for the past
thirty years.

   A. Job equality has been a requirement in government contracts
since 1941, when F.D.R. passed it into law.[1]

      1. Penalty for noncompliance is cancellation of the
contract.[2]

      2. In thirty years, not one contract has ever been cancelled.[3]

   B. One out of every three jobs is due to government contracts
with private corporations.[4]

II. Trade unions have failed to end job discrimination to the extent
that they could.

A. Existing apprenticeship programs prevent minority groups from entering certain trades.

B. Certain government-sponsored plans have proved ineffective.

    1. "Chicago Plan"[5]

    2. "Outreach Program"[6]

Conclusion:

The federal government and large trade unions needed to evaluate their role in adding to the burden of the Black American through economic discrimination. Steps could then be taken to be sure that all Americans are given opportunities for economic progress, security, and personal growth.

[* Note: The superior numbers indicate the use and order of the student's note cards.]

Application

Now you are ready to shape your material into an outline. Here is a good procedure to follow.

Objective: To prepare a sentence outline for your paper.

Procedure:

1. Work with your note cards until you have organized them in the best possible way.

2. Go through the ordered note cards, organizing the ideas in outline form and expressing each idea in a complete sentence.

3. Check your note cards to be sure they are in the same order as your outline. Then number the note cards consecutively and write the number of each card in the appropriate place in your outline.

Step 12—Writing Several Drafts

Application

Now that you have completed your outline, you are ready to write your research paper. You will probably have to rewrite the paper several times. You may find that some sections need many revisions to make them sound right. At this point you might wish to read Appendix A, which will give you detailed instruction in the entire composing process. After each draft refer to the Self-Evaluation Guide in Appendix D for help in judging your own work critically.

Objective: To write as many drafts and revisions of your paper as are necessary to satisfy *you.* (Of course, the higher *your* standards are, the better your paper will be.)

Procedure:

1. The First Draft—Composing: The aim of the first draft is to turn your outline into smoothly flowing prose in which the sentences in the outline have been expanded, added to, and linked together. It may help you at this point to refer to the list of transitional words and phrases in Appendix C. When you use sentences from your outline that are followed by numbers (those that refer to note cards), be sure to transfer the numbers to your draft. As you work, concentrate on getting your ideas down with good style. Do not expect to compose the first draft in just one writing session. Most writers continually revise as they write. They rework sentences, change paragraphs, and often get stuck on a particular section, which they rework again and again. You can always use focused free writing and brainstorming as aids for your actual writing. Do not concern yourself with grammar, spelling, punctuation (called surface features) at this point.

2. The Second Draft: The aim of writing a second draft is to polish and perfect your paper. Reread your first draft critically. You can do this better if you wait a day or two between writing the first draft and rereading it. Revise all of those sections that you can improve. Some parts of the paper may need several revisions;

some may need none. When you revise you should be focusing on the clarity, meaning, and power of your writing. If anything you have written seems unclear or awkward to you, the writer, chances are the reader will feel the same way. Be sure to revise all of those sections that you "feel" are weak. Do not concern yourself with surface features yet.

3. The Third Draft—Editing: After you have revised your paper, you are ready to edit. At this point you are going to correct your paper for grammar, spelling, punctuation, and all other surface errors. In order to edit correctly, you must read your paper very slowly, several times and aloud if possible. Try to pace each editing of your paper several hours apart. As you reread your paper, correct the errors you find, consulting your dictionary, thesaurus, and grammar book when necessary. It is most important not to worry about surface errors until you have completed the composing and revising process. Writers who worry about surface features too soon find that their flow of ideas is hampered.

4. Additional Drafts: Many writers find they need additional drafts as they move through composing, revising, and editing. Keep reworking your paper until you are satisfied. When you think you are ready to write a final draft, you should proceed to Step 13 so that you will be able to include your footnotes at the same time.

Step 13—Footnoting; The Final Draft

In writing your paper, you have depended upon facts, ideas, and opinions gathered in the course of your research. Every writer is under an obligation to point out the places where he depends on the words or thinking of someone else and to cite the person whose work he is using. The single exception to this practice is material that is common knowledge. It is, of course, impossible to say exactly what constitutes common knowledge in a particular field. But certainly ideas and information that you have come across repeatedly in your research and have found in several different sources can be regarded as such. There will be many borderline cases. In the papers you write for your courses, it is perhaps the safest practice to footnote when in doubt.

The form footnotes take depends on the area of research. The social sciences, the natural sciences and the humanities each require slightly different forms. For each of these areas there are documentation guidelines available in college and public libraries. *The Publication Manual of the American Psychological Association* is used for the social sciences. *The Handbook for Authors*, published by the American Chemical Society, is used for scientific papers. *The Modern Language Association Handbook* is used for the humanities. In addition, many instructors provide students with a style guide for their particular course. You must make sure to ask your instructor which documentation form is required for your paper. This applies to bibliographical forms as well as footnotes. In this book, all of the forms used are based on *The Modern Language Association Handbook*.

A footnote reference consists of two parts: a marker in the text, usually a small raised number; and the footnote itself, identified with a corresponding number and usually placed at the bottom of the page. In the paper you are writing, you should place footnotes at the bottom of the appropriate page and number them consecutively throughout. When you are typing your paper, you will need to plan ahead in order to have room for the footnotes.

The proper footnoting of your paper began when you were doing your research and making out bibliography cards and note cards. The process continued as you carried the numbers of your note cards from your outline through the various drafts of your paper. When you are ready to do the final draft, it is time to expand these numbers into footnotes. This is done by using the number in the text to locate the original note card and using the reference on the note card to locate the relevant bibliography card. All of the information you need to write a footnote will be found on these two cards: the description of the source on the bibliography card and the specific page number on the note card.

The form of a footnote is also important. Forms for three different kinds of sources are given in the Presentation below. Forms for other kinds of sources can be found in Appendix B. If you are going to be referring to the same source more than once in your paper, it will save you time to use short forms, which are also explained in Appendix B.

Presentation

Following are three footnotes. After each footnote, you will find the bibliography card and the note card from which the footnote information was taken. The forms for these and other kinds of footnotes can be found in Appendix B.

1. Footnote entry for a book:

[1] David Stevens, <u>Patterns of Population Growth</u> (Hartsdale, N.Y.: Sydney Mark, Inc., 1989), p. 39.

Stevens, David

<u>Patterns of Population Growth</u>

Hartsdale, N.Y.

Sydney Mark, Inc.

1989

---

future population   39

Stevens

The rate of population growth may decline in the future but the actual numbers of persons may increase.

Example I: U.S. population =
            1980 rate of growth
            less but actually
            more people—
            200 million +

2. Footnote entry for an article:

[2] Bea Edelson, ''Reconstructing Custer,'' <u>American History Quarterly</u>, 42 (Spring 1986), pp. 153, 154.

Edelson, Bea

"Reconstructing Custer"

<u>American History Quarterly</u>

42

Spring 1986

pgs. 150-163

Soldiers, number

153, 154

Edelson

I. Numbers of active participants in last battle

Indians = 1105

Custer = 136

3. Footnote entry for an anonymous article:

³ ''Emerson's Debt to the Baghavad-Gita,''
Cultural Exchange Journal, 4 (Sept, 1988),
p. 57.

Anonymous

"Emerson's Debt to the Baghavad-Gita"

Cultural Exchange Journal

4

Sept. 1988

pgs. 56-71

57

Emerson's
poems and
the Gita

"Emerson's Debt to the
Baghavad-Gita"

Several stanzas of the Gita
are found in Emerson's poem
"Brahma" in practically a
word for word translation.

Application

This Application should be done at the same time as the final draft of the paper.

Objective: To prepare footnotes for your paper that are correct in form and content.

Procedure:

1. As you do the final draft, turn the numbers in the text into footnotes, getting the necessary information from your note cards and bibliography cards and using the forms given in Appendix B. Number the footnotes consecutively throughout the paper.

2. Omit footnotes for any material that can fairly be called common knowledge.

3. Whenever possible, use short forms as explained in Appendix B.

4. Type the footnotes at the bottom of the appropriate pages, separating them from the last line of the text by a double space, a line about 1½ inches long (use the underscore key), and another double space. Indent the first line of each footnote five spaces. Type footnote numbers slightly above the line.

Step 14—Preparing the Bibliography

The bibliography is an alphabetical listing of all of the sources you have used in writing your paper. As with footnotes, the social sciences, the natural sciences, and the humanities each require different bibliographical forms. The same documentation guidelines mentioned in Step 13 should be used for your bibliography. Again, the following examples are taken from *The Modern Language Association Handbook*. Your bibliography should be fairly easy to prepare because most of the work was done during the research process when you made out your bibliography cards. In fact, the bibliography can be typed directly from the cards. The Presentation below gives the correct forms for three kinds of sources. Forms for other kinds of sources can be found in Appendix B.

Presentation

Below are three bibliography entries followed by the cards from which they were taken.

1. Bibliography entry for a book:

Weinstein, Rosalie <u>The History of the American Frontier</u>. New York: Russell and Russell, 1988.

Weinstein, Rosalie

<u>The History of the American Frontier</u>

New York
Russell and Russell
1988

2. Bibliography entry for an article:

Gittelson, Ellen. ''Modern Music's Symbols.''
<u>Music Digest</u>, 6 (Spring, 1986), 39–47.

Gittelson, Ellen

"Modern Music's Symbols"

<u>Music Digest</u>

6

Spring 1986

pgs. 39 to 47

3. Bibliography entry for an anonymous article:

''New York's Newest Union.'' <u>New York Today</u>, 4
(April 10, 1985), 41–50.

Anonymous

   "New York's Newest Union"

   <u>New York Today</u>

   4
   April 10, 1985
   pgs. 41 to 50

Application

The bibliography will be the last section of your paper. As with footnotes, it is important to give the information accurately and to maintain good form. The following procedure will help you do this.

Objective: To prepare a bibliography for your paper that is correct in form and content.

Procedure:

1. Take all of your bibliography cards and arrange them in alphabetical order according to the author's last name; or where there is no author, the first word of the title (ignoring *a, an,* and *the*).

2. Type the entries directly from the cards, using the forms given in Appendix B. If an entry takes more than one line, the second and subsequent lines should be indented, usually five spaces. Be sure to match the commas, the underlining, and the spacing that are shown in Appendix B.

Step 15—Creating a Title

Application

Now is the time to start thinking about a final title for your paper. Perhaps you have had a title in mind for some time. In that case, the following procedure will give you a chance to consider other possibilities.

Objective: To create a title that will be suitable for your paper.

Procedure:

1. Think about your topic, your thesis, and the final draft of your paper. Then think of at least three titles that you could use. One might be explanatory, telling what is in the paper; another might be more fanciful, trying to catch the spirit of what you have

done. Don't give up too easily on this. You should spend at least fifteen minutes trying to get some fresh ideas.

2. Of the titles you have thought of, select the one that you feel will be most suitable for your paper.

Step 16—Typing and Proofreading the Paper

Application

Once you have completed a final draft with footnotes in place, it is time to think of the final typing of the paper. The following procedure will give you some useful guidelines.

Objective: To produce a final paper that is accurate and attractive.

Procedure:

1. Use 8½-by-11-inch paper. Leave a margin of 1 inch at the top and bottom and of 1¼ inches at each side.

2. Double-space the entire paper with the following exceptions:

   (a) single-space within individual footnotes and bibliography entries, but double-space between footnotes and bibliography entries.

   (b) a long quotation should be single-spaced and given extra indention at both right and left. Here is an example:

It is necessary to develop a concept of the Hindu ''Brahma.'' This element is basic to any study of Hindu philosophy and its application to morality is most interesting:

> ''Brahma'' in the ancient Hindu sense, refers to supreme all-pervading spirit of life. This spirit is the activating life force. It is eternal non-divisible, non-destructible, non-creatable.[16]

Emerson took this concept, Yankee-fied it, and brought it to popularity.

---

3. Indent the first line of each paragraph and footnote five spaces. Indent every line of a bibliography entry five spaces except the first line, which starts at the margin.

4. Center page numbers at the top of the page or place them in the upper right-hand corner.

5. Place footnotes at the bottom of the appropriate pages. Between text and footnote, double-space, type a line about 1½ inches long, and double-space again.

6. Always make at least one copy of your paper, either a carbon or a machine copy, because sometimes papers are lost.

7. You are not going to be judged on your skill as a typist, and the final copy need not be letter-perfect. It should be carefully proofread or edited and any mistakes neatly corrected. Here are some commonly used proofreading marks that you may find helpful:

   ⁊   indicates that a new paragaph should begin.

   ∧   indicates where something is to be inserted.

        a   *am*

      ppper   I going home

   ∿   indicates that letters or words should be reversed

        research   New City York

   For other errors, cross out the mistake neatly with *one* line only, and write the correct version in the space above the error.

8. Now is the time to give everything a last-minute check. Do you have all the parts: cover page, text, bibliography, possibly illustrations or other supplementary material? When you have everything together in the right order, you can place it in a plastic see-through binder, which will protect your work and add to its appearance.

[Note: Many students are now using a word processor when they write papers. Many programs will enable you to do all of Section Three, "Writing the Paper," on a computer. The basic step-by-step procedure is the same, but using a processor will certainly make the task much easier.]

APPENDIX

A—The Composing Process

•

In the past decade much research has been done to discover how people write effectively. On the basis of this research, writing teachers have developed several strategies to help students improve and enjoy their writing. Using these strategies should help you as you go through the steps of writing a research paper.

1. Prewriting: Before most writers actually begin writing, they think about what they are going to do. There are several techniques that help students record their thinking so that they can eventually use their ideas in an organized way.

   a. Free writing: This technique helps writers "loosen up" and connect their ideas to paper. This is very much like the warm-up exercises athletes do before a workout. The procedure is simple. Take a pencil and paper (good size, 8½-by-11) and write down all of your thoughts during a ten-minute period. Just let your ideas and your pencil flow freely without stopping. When you reread your free writing you will be surprised how much it reveals about your concerns and feelings. Many writers keep their free writing in a journal as a record of self-discovery. In addition, students who free write regularly show marked improvement in their writing, especially in what they do for school.

   b. Focused free writing: This technique uses the ten-minute nonstop writing a little differently. The writer now focuses his free writing on a particular subject. When writing a research paper, students use this technique to develop a topic by focusing on the area of research, to develop an idea sheet by focusing on their topic, or to work out difficulties in the initial drafts of their paper by focusing on the section giving them trouble. Students are always finding new ways to use focused free writing to help them with their academic work.

c. Brainstorming and Listing: These techniques are another way of prewriting, which records ideas that the writer will later develop. They require the writer to free-associate and record his responses to a particular topic, idea, word, or phrase.

The writer writes his topic, idea, word, or phrase in the middle of the page and surrounds it with all of the words and phrases he thinks of as connected to his central point. Then he lists columns of all of the ideas that seem to belong together. On page 53, you will find an example of brainstorming and listing used to develop a topic from a research area about the American labor movement.

Brainstorming and Listing

strike

depression

U. F. T.

teachers

AREA OF RESEARCH

American Labor Movement

steel workers

air traffic controllers

1930s

teamsters

paraprofessionals

Listings

U. F. T.

teachers

paraprofessionals

strike

new unions

1930s depression

Topic

How the paraprofessionals working for the N.Y.C. Board of Education became part of the U. F. T.

2. Composing and Revising: You, the writer, should use prewriting strategies until you feel you have discovered something you want to write about. Then you begin actually composing. At this point you should try to get your ideas written out in such a way that they are clear, logically organized, meaningful, interesting, and powerful. Do not worry about grammar, spelling, punctuation, and other surface errors when you are composing. Concern with these surface features often stops the flow of ideas. You will have time to correct or edit your errors after you have finished composing. As you write, you will often want to make changes. You may decide to use a different word, change a sentence, rework a paragraph, or change the order in which you originally composed. Making these kinds of changes is called revising. Revisions involve: meaning of your writing, clarity, organization, and style. Most writers compose and revise many times as they work. It is rare for a writer to sit down and write from beginning to end and never change anything. If you find you revise and rework your paper many times, you are probably doing a better and better job. The best judge of when to revise is often you, the writer. If you sense that something you have written does not sound as you would like it, revise it!

3. Editing: After you have revised your paper to your satisfaction, it is time to edit. Now you should read your paper, aloud if possible, very slowly. Focus on the surface features—grammar, spelling, punctuation. It is necessary to edit more than once and to space the editing over several hours or even days. Have a dictionary, thesaurus, and basic grammar book handy as you edit. Always edit one final time just before you hand in your paper. Most instructors welcome a few corrections, neatly done, even on the final copy of a paper.

B—DOCUMENTATION

When you write a research paper, you use facts, ideas, and opinions from many sources. Unless this information is common knowledge in the field about which you are writing, you should give credit to the author, regardless of whether you have used his words exactly (direct quote) or expressed his ideas in your own words (paraphrase). This citation of sources also makes it possible for the reader to investigate the matters you have written about for himself.

The system by which a writer acknowledges his indebtedness to others is called documentation. For a research paper, documentation takes two forms: (1) a bibliography in which you list alphabetically all of the sources you have consulted; and (2) footnotes, which are specific acknowledgments attached to the appropriate parts of the text. Both bibliography and footnotes should be given in a standard form. This appendix on documentation is designed as a quick reference that you can consult whenever you need to know what the standard forms are.

Alternate Form for Footnotes and Bibliographies

Remember—the forms used in this book are based on *The Modern Language Association Handbook,* which is used mainly in humanities courses. This book also uses the long form of footnotes found in the handbook, but there is also a shorter, internal footnote form that some instructors prefer. This footnote uses the author's name and page enclosed in parentheses within the body of the paper itself, and the reader must refer to the bibliography for the full citation. Such a footnote for this book would look like this (Cash 62). If several works by the same author need to be cited in the paper, then a shortened title is used. An example of this would be: (Cash, *How to Write a Research Paper,* 62). See page 57 for an example of how these internal footnotes would look if used on a page of the sample paper in Appendix B:

If you are writing your paper for a social science or natural science course, be sure to check with your instructor as to the form you should use for both footnotes and bibliography. Two guidebooks for research writers are *The Publication Manual of the American Psychological Association,* for the social sciences; and *The Handbook for Authors,* published by the American Chemical Society, for the natural sciences. Both of these guidebooks can be found in college or public libraries.

Footnotes—General Rules

1. The first line of each footnote is indented five spaces from the left-hand margin. The subsequent lines begin at the left-hand margin.

2. Each footnote should be single-spaced, with a double space between footnotes.

3. The footnotes themselves can be placed at the bottom of the page where the information from the source cited appears. They can also be placed in a list arranged in order of use in the paper. Sometimes footnotes are placed within the paper itself in an abbreviated form. Be sure to ask your instructor which method is preferred. For the sample paper in this book, the footnotes will be placed at the bottom of the page. When you type these footnotes, double-space after the last line of text, type a line about 1½ inches long, double-space again, and begin your footnotes. Be sure you are consistent and use the same form throughout the paper.

not even an out-house. The front yards are frequently littered with abandoned, broken-down automobiles that are too expensive to repair and too much trouble to junk (Sorkin 1).

The largest settlement on the reservation contains the Office of the Bureau of Indian Affairs and the hospital, which is operated by the U.S. Public Health Service. The large modern homes of the government employees stand in shocking contrast to the shacks of the Indians. The stores in the town are small but fairly modern. Very few Indians are employed in them, and few are Indian-owned or managed (Sorkin 1-2).

The walls and shelves of the reservation trading post are lined with silver and turquoise articles as well as family treasures pawned by Indians who will never save

Forms for Footnotes

A footnote contains the author's name, the title, publication information, and the exact pages on which you found the information you've used in your paper. This data appears in the following order:

For a Book:

1. Author's first name, middle initial (if given), last name; then a comma; then:
2. The title of the book, underlined; then:
3. Open parenthesis, place of publication; then a colon; then:
4. The name of the publisher; then a comma; then:
5. The year of publication; then close parenthesis; then a comma; then:
6. The exact pages on which the information you used originally appeared; then a period.

For an Article:

1. Author's first name, middle initial (if given), last name; then a comma; then:
2. The title of the article in quotation marks, with a comma before the closing quotation marks; then:
3. The name of the periodical in which the article appeared, underlined; then a comma; then:
4. The date the periodical appeared; then a comma; then:
5. All of the pages on which the information you have used appeared; then a period.

In addition to these standard forms for a book and an article, there are special forms for different types of sources. The most common are shown below. Using these examples and the general rules, you should be able to write correct footnotes for any sources you use.

Anonymous Work

Book:

[1] Indian Lands (New York: Genn Publishing Co., 1989), pp. 16–17.

Article:

[2] ''The U.F.T. and the Schools,'' Life, 44 (October 5, 1985), p. 44.

Anthology

[3] Steve S. David, ''The Migrant Puerto Rican,'' in Modern Population Movement, ed. Mark Syd (Calif.: Ben Press, 1959), p. 472.

Editor of a collection

[4] Janet Allen, ed., Selected Lyrics from the Age of Rock (London: New Sounds Press, 1965), p. 35.

Encyclopedia and Dictionaries

[5] ''Ralph Waldo Emerson,'' Encyclopedia of Biography (1925), V, 440.

Interview

[6] Dr. Lewis Burrows, Personal interview, Mt. Sinai Hospital, New York, N.Y., June 3, 1988.

Letter

[7] Anya Ben-Theo, Personal letter, March 13, 1985.

Lecture

[8] Denise Totah, Lecture: ''Oriental Design in Emerson's Poetry,'' Columbia University, New York, N.Y., October 5, 1974.

Multiple Authors

Two or three authors:

[9] Mark Korn, Syd Stevens, and Ceil Kusin, <u>An Approach to the Brahmans</u>, 4th ed. (New York: Appleby and Sons, 1944), pp. 45—46.

More than three authors:

[10] Dr. Ben Lapkin, et al., <u>Praise the Beatles</u> (London: Simon and Schuster, 1969), p. 108.

Newspaper

No article title or author:

[11] <u>New York Times</u>, June 3, 1935, Sec. 4, p. 10.

Article title and author:

[12] Maury Allen, ''A Growing Union,'' <u>New York Eagle</u>, March 20, 1976, Sec. 2, p. 45.

Article title, no author:

[13] ''The Puerto Rican Melting Pot,'' <u>Miami Post</u>, March 14, 1952, p. 5.

Pamphlet

Organization as author:

[14] University of the State of New York, State Education Department, <u>Collective Bargaining for the Paraprofessional</u> (Albany, 1968), pp. 28—29.

No author:

¹⁵ <u>Indian Land Treaties</u> (Washington, D.C.:
1875), p. 15.

Unpublished Work

¹⁶ Millicent Lapkin, ''A Study of Female
Puerto Rican Migration to New York City''
(Unpublished thesis, Lehman College, 1989),
p. 5.

Short Forms

There are two short forms you can use when you are citing a source for a second time. They are called consecutive and nonconsecutive citations. Suppose you have used a source in your paper and have written a footnote according to previous instructions. Then you find that you are using the same source immediately again, or consecutively. For this second citation you may use the Latin Ibid., meaning "in the same place." Your first citation of the source and the use of Ibid. would look like this:

[1] Phyllis Cash, Emerson, An American Puzzle (New York: Simon and Schuster, 1986), p. 45.

[2] Ibid.

If you have used a different page of the same source, then the second footnote would look like this:

[2] Ibid., p. 49.

Now suppose that you use this same source again, but this time after having used several other sources. Now you need the short form for a nonconsecutive citation. This consists of the author's last name, a comma, and the page of the citation. The nonconsecutive citation would look like this:

[9] Cash, p. 106.

If you have used two or more books by the same author, you must include the title of the source in the nonconsecutive citation:

[11] Cash, American Poets, p. 56.

If you use these short forms, you will never have to write a complete footnote for any source more than once.

Bibliography—General Rules

1. Each bibliography entry begins at the left-hand margin. Each subsequent line is indented (usually five spaces).

2. Each entry should be single-spaced, with a double-space between entries.

3. Bibliography entries are arranged alphabetically by the author's last name. Sometimes an organization, government agency, or committee may be considered the author of an item. If there is no author, the entry is listed by the first word of the title, excluding the articles (a, an, the).

4. If you are listing two or more items by the same author, you may use a horizontal line about one inch long (use the hyphen key) instead of the author's name in all entries after the first. For example:

Cash, Phyllis. <u>Emerson, An American Puzzle</u>. New York: Simon & Schuster, 1986.

_____.<u>Hindu Influence in America</u>. New York: Simon & Schuster, 1989.

5. Bibliography entries are usually *not* numbered.

6. Bibliographies usually have an appropriate title such as "A Selected Bibliography."

Forms for Bibliography Entries

The bibliography entry contains the author's name, the title, and publication information in the following order:

For a Book:

1. Author's last name; then a comma; the author's first name and initial (if given); then a period; then:

2. The title of the book, underlined; then a period; then:

3. The place of publication; then a colon; then:

4. The name of the publisher; then a comma; then:

5. The year of publication; then a period.

For an Article:

1. Author's last name; then a comma; the author's first name and initial (if given); then a period; then:

2. The title of the article in quotation marks, with a period before the closing quotation marks; then:

3. The name of the periodical in which the article appeared, underlined; then a comma; then:

4. The date the periodical appeared; then a comma; then:

5. All of the pages on which the article appeared; then a period.

As with footnotes, there are special forms for different types of sources. The examples below are the bibliographical entries for the same sources used in the footnote examples.

Anonymous Work

Book:

Indian Lands. New York: Genn Publishing Co., 1989.

Article:

''The U.F.T. and the Schools,'' <u>Life</u>, 44
(October 5, 1985): 44–48.

Anthology

David, Steve S. ''The Migrant Puerto Rican'' in
<u>Modern Population Movement</u>. ed. Mark Syd.
Calif.: Ben Press, 1959.

Editor of a Collection

Allen, Janet, ed. <u>Selected Lyrics from the Age
of Rock</u>. London: New Sounds Press, 1965.

Encyclopedia and Dictionaries

''Ralph Waldo Emerson.'' <u>Encyclopedia of
Biography</u>. (1925), V, 439–441.

Interview

Burrows, Dr. Lewis. Personal interview on
Puerto Rican workers in a New York City
hospital. Mt. Sinai Hospital, New York, N.Y.,
June 3, 1988.

Letter

Ben-Theo, Anya. Personal letter. March 13,
1985.

Lecture

Totah, Denise. Lecture: ''Oriental Design in
Emerson's Poetry.'' Columbia University, New
York, N.Y., October 5, 1974.

Multiple Authors

Two or three authors:

Korn, Mark, Syd Stevens, and Ceil Kusin. <u>An Approach to the Brahmans</u>. 4th ed. New York: Appleby and Sons, 1944.

More than three authors:

Lapkin, Dr. Ben, et al. <u>Praise the Beatles</u>. London: Simon and Schuster, 1969.

Newspaper

No article title or author:

<u>New York Times</u>. June 3, 1935, Sec. 4, 10.

Article title and author:

Allen, Maury. ''A Growing Union,'' <u>New York Eagle</u>. March 20, 1976, Sec. 2, 45–51.

Article title, no author:

''Puerto Rican Melting Pot, The,'' <u>Miami Post</u>. March 14, 1952, 5, 8–10.

Pamphlet

Organization as author:

University of the State of New York, State Education Department. <u>Collective Bargaining for the Paraprofessional</u>. Albany: 1968.

No author:

Indian Land Treaties. Washington, D.C.: 1875.

Unpublished Work

Lapkin, Millicent. ''A Study of Female Puerto
    Rican Migration to New York City.''
    Unpublished thesis. Lehman College, 1989.

Salvatore L. Scorzello
ACS 110—8
April 10, 1989

THE CONDITION OF THE AMERICAN INDIAN
An Overview—1490s to 1970s

Professor Phyllis Cash

THE CONDITION OF AMERICAN INDIANS

Poverty in the United States of America is not uncommon, nor is it partial to any race, creed, or color. However, when we look back into the history of America, we can find a case of severe destitution and want, concerning not just a group of people but a whole race—an Indian race of people who were rich in food, shelter, and land at one time. A land which we call ours today is the United States of America, but in the truest sense of the word, it is ''stolen property'' for, in fact, the United States government took the land from the Indians and impoverished them.

It began with Christopher Columbus, who gave the people the name Indios. He described them as peace-loving, generous people. As it is quoted, he wrote to the King and Queen of Spain, ''that I swear to your Majesties there is not in the world a better nation. They love their neighbors as themselves, and their discourse is ever sweet and gentle, and accompanied with a smile; and though it is true that they are naked yet their manners are decorous and praiseworthy.''[1]

---

[1] Dee Brown, Bury My Heart at Wounded Knee (New York: Holt, Rinehart and Winston, 1970), p. 1.

But, unfortunately, their ways were considered a sign of weakness and the Europeans soon took advantage and undertook to enforce their ways upon the people of the New World. The Europeans could have learned something about their own relationship to the earth from a people who were true conservationists.

Columbus kidnapped ten of his friendly Taino Indians and carried them off to Spain, where they could be introduced to the white man's ways. Spaniards looted and burned villages and kidnapped hundreds of men, women, and children so they could be shipped to Europe and sold as slaves. The Taino and Arawak tribes began to resist, thus bringing on the use of guns and sabers, and whole tribes were destroyed—hundreds of thousands of people in less than a decade after Columbus set foot on the beach of San Salvador, October 12, 1492.[2]

When the English-speaking white men arrived in Virginia in 1607, they used subtler methods to ensure peace with the Powhatans who resided there. They made a gold crown for Chief Wahunsona-cook and placed it upon his head naming him King Powhatan and convinced him to put his people to work supplying the white settlers with food. After Wahunsona-cook died, the Powhatans rose up in revenge to drive the Englishmen back into the sea from which they had come, but the Indians underestimated the power of English weapons. In a short time, the eight thousand Powhatans

---

[2] _Ibid_., p. 2.

were reduced to less than a thousand.[3] In each state, they began somewhat differently but ended virtually the same as in Virginia.

In Massachusetts and up and down the Pemaquid land which we now call New England, the settlers were coming by the thousands. So, in 1625, some of the colonists asked Chief Samoset to give them 12,000 additional acres of Pemaquid land. Samoset knew that the land came from the Great Spirit and belonged to no man. Believing that the land was as endless as the sky, he decided to humor these strangers in their strange ways, and went through a ceremony of transferring the land and made his mark on a paper for them. It was the first deed of Indian land to English colonists.[4]

Most of the other settlers did not bother to go through such a ceremony. By the time Massasoit, great Chief of the Wampanoags, died in 1662, his people were pushed even further back into the wilderness. His son, Metacom, named King Philip by the New Englanders, led his tribe and others in a war against the white man in 1675 to save his and other tribes from extinction. But, once again, the firepower of the colonists destroyed thousands of Indians and virtually exterminated the Wampanoag and Narragansett tribes. King Philip was killed and his head publicly exhibited at Plymouth for twenty years. Along with other captured Indian women

---

[3] <u>Ibid</u>., p. 3.

[4] <u>Ibid</u>., p. 3.

and children, his wife and young son were sold into slavery in the West Indies.[5]

For more than two centuries, these events were repeated again and again as the European colonists moved inland through the passes of the Alleghenies and down the westward-flowing rivers to the Great Waters (the Mississippi) and then up the Great Muddy (the Missouri).[6]

The Five Nations of the Iroquois, mightiest and most advanced of all eastern tribes, strove in vain for peace. After years of bloodshed to save their political independence, they finally went down in defeat. Some escaped to Canada, some fled westward, some lived out their lives in reservation confinement.[7]

During the 1760s, Pontiac of the Ottawas united tribes in the Great Lakes country in hopes of driving the British back across the Alleghenies, but he failed.[8]

A generation later, Tecumseh of the Shawnees formed a great confederacy of midwestern and southern tribes to protect their lands from invasion. The dream ended with Tecumseh's death in battle during the War of 1812.[9]

Finally, in 1829, Andrew Jackson, who was called Sharp Knife by the Indians, took office as President of the United States. In his first

---

[5] *Ibid.*, p. 3.
[6] *Ibid.*, p. 4.
[7] *Ibid.*, p. 4.
[8] *Ibid.*, p. 4.
[9] *Ibid.*, p. 4.

message to the Congress, he recommended that all Indians be removed westward beyond the Mississippi. ''I suggest the propriety of setting apart an ample district west of the Mississippi . . . to be guaranteed to the Indian tribes, as long as they shall occupy it.''[10]

Although enactment of such a law would only add to the long list of broken promises made to the eastern Indians, Sharp Knife was convinced that Indians and whites could not live together in peace and that his plan would make possible a final promise which never would be broken again. On May 28, 1830, Sharp Knife's recommendations became law.[11]

Before these laws could be put into effect, a new wave of white settlers swept westward and the policymakers in Washington shifted the ''permanent Indian frontier'' from the Mississippi River to the 95th meridian. (This line ran from Lake of the Woods on what is now the Minnesota—Canada border).[12]

The decade following the establishment of the ''permanent Indian frontier'' was a bad time for the eastern tribes. The great Cherokee nation had survived more than a hundred years of the white man's wars, diseases, and whiskey, but when gold was discovered within their Appalachian territory, their removal to the West, which was planned in gradual stages, became an immedi-

---

[10] Ibid., p. 5.
[11] Ibid., p. 5.
[12] Ibid., p. 6.

ate wholesale exodus. In 1838, General Winfield Scott's soldiers rounded them up and concentrated them into camps. A few hundred escaped to the Smoky Mountains and many years later were given a small reservation in North Carolina. From the prison camps they were led westward to Indian Territory. On the long winter trek, one out of every four Cherokees died from cold, hunger, or disease. They called their march their ''trail of tears.''[13]

Scarcely were the refugees settled in their so-called ''permanent Indian frontier'' when the United States went to war with Mexico. When the war ended in 1847, the United States took possession of a vast expanse of territory reaching from Texas to California. All of it was west of the ''permanent Indian frontier.''[14]

Throughout the land, promises made by the white man were broken, even after signing peace treaties with the Indians. One particular example occurred in the spring of 1868. The Great Warrior Sherman (General Sherman) and Red Cloud (leader of the Sioux) agreed to sign a peace treaty after a war that had gone on for more than two years: ''From this day forward all war between the parties to this agreement shall forever cease. The government of the United States desires peace, and its honor is hereby pledged to keep it. The

---

[13] Ibid., pp. 7–8.
[14] Ibid., p. 8.

Indians desire peace, and they now pledge their honor to maintain it.''[15]

For the next twenty years, however, the contents of the other sixteen articles of the treaty of 1868 would remain a matter of dispute between the Indians and the government of the United States. What many of the chiefs understood was in the treaty and what was actually written therein after Congress ratified it were like two horses whose colorations did not match. (Spotted Tail, nine years later: ''These promises have not been kept. . . . All the words have proved to be false. . . . There was a treaty made by General Sherman, General Sanborn, and General Harney. At that time the general told us we should have annuities and goods from that treaty for thirty-five years. He said this but yet he didn't tell the truth.''[16]

Consequently, our half million American Indians are living today on reservations. An Indian reservation can be characterized as an open-air slum. It has a feeling of emptiness and isolation. There are miles and miles of dirt or gravel roads without any signs of human life. The scattered Indian communities are made up of scores of tarpaper shacks or log cabins with one tiny window and a stovepipe sticking out of a roof that is weighted down with pieces of metal and automobile tires. Each of these dwellings, called homes, have as many as six or seven

---

[15] Ibid., pp. 140–141.
[16] Ibid., pp. 141–142.

people living in them. Some of the homes have no electricity or running water—sometimes not even an outhouse. The front yards are frequently littered with abandoned, broken-down automobiles that are too expensive to repair and too much trouble to junk.[17]

The largest settlement on the reservation contains the office of the Bureau of Indian Affairs and the hospital, which is operated by the U.S. Public Health Service. The large modern homes of the government employees stand in shocking contrast to the shacks of the Indians. The stores in the town are small but fairly modern. Very few Indians are employed in them, and few are Indian-owned or managed.[18]

The walls and shelves of the reservation trading post are lined with silver and turquoise articles as well as family treasures pawned by Indians who will never save enough money to reclaim them. Most of the items for sale have no price tags. What better way to keep the Indian rug weavers or silversmiths who sell to the traders from learning the real vàlue of their work? The number of unemployed is striking. Everywhere, there seem to be dozens of Indians standing or sitting around doing nothing. With so much time on their hands, many pass the day drinking in bars just outside the reservation.[19]

---

[17] Alan L. Sorkin, _American Indians and Federal Aid_ (Washington, D.C.: The Brookings Institution, 1971), p. 1.

[18] _Ibid_., p. 1-2.

[19] _Ibid_., p. 2.

Indians are, in general, stoic people. They have learned to accept in silence the burdens of suffering brought about by white domination. They wait hours to see the Indian service doctor and to meet with a Bureau of Indian Affairs official to discuss payment of income from Indian lands leased to whites. The Indians seldom complain about the wait or the lack of chairs or the indifference with which they are treated by the white officials.[20]

A survey taken in 1970 showed that the vast majority of American Indians live in abject poverty; 74% of reservation families earned less than $3,000 a year (the poverty threshold). While their income rose considerably more between 1939 and 1969 than that of the total population, it was a little more than half of the latter's in 1969, as shown in the table on page 10.[21]

The table also shows a widening gap between reservation and non-reservation Indians. In 1949, the median income of the Indians on reservations was 80% of the income of those living elsewhere; in 1959, the figure had dropped to 60%. The increased disparity results from the migration of many relatively well-educated and highly skilled Indians to major urban centers during the 1950s. In the metropolitan areas, better-paying jobs, more commensurate with their level of ability, were available, while the reservation economy remained comparatively stagnant.

---

[20] Ibid., p. 2.
[21] Ibid., p. 8.

10
Median Income for Male Indians, Blacks, and Whites, 1939–1969[22]
(*1969 Dollars*)

Year	All Indians	Urban Indians	Reservation Indians	Blacks	Whites
1939	—	—	$ 576	$1,066	$2,035
1944	—	—	760	1,843	3,506
1949	$1,094	$1,198	950	2,218	3,780
1959	2,218	2,961	1,699	3,398	5,229
1964	—	—	2,074	3,947	6,743
1969	3,509	4,568	2,603	4,508	7,579
Percentage Increase 1939–1969	—	—	352	323	281
Percentage Increase 1949–1969	220	281	174	103	105

Source: U.S. Department of Commerce, Bureau of the Census, *Income of Families and Persons in the United States* (*1965*), *Current Population Reports* Series P-60, nos. 5, 7, and pp. 41–51 in no. 47; U.S. Department of Interior, Bureau of Indian Affairs, "Reservation Income, 1939" (Washington, D.C.: 1939), unpublished; U.S. Department of Commerce, Bureau of the Census, 1940 Census of Population, *The Labor Force* (Washington, D.C.: U.S. Government Printing Office, 1943), table 71, p. 116; U.S. Department of Commerce, Bureau of the Census, 1940 Census of Population, *Education* (Washington, D.C.: U.S. Government Printing Office, 1943), table 31, p. 161; U.S. Department of Commerce, Bureau of the Census, 1950 Census of Population, *Nonwhite Population by Race* (Washington, D.C.: U.S. Government Printing Office, 1953), table 10, p. 32 and table 21, p. 72; U.S. Department of Commerce, Bureau of the Census, 1950 Census of Population, *Occupational Characteristics* (Washington, D.C.: U.S. Government Printing Office, 1956), table 10, p. 183 and table 21, p. 215; U.S. Department of Commerce, Bureau of the Census, 1960 Census of Population, *Nonwhite Population by Race* (Washington, D.C.: U.S. Government Printing Office, 1963), table 33, p. 104; U.S. Department of Commerce, Bureau of the Census, 1960 Census of Population, *Occupational Characteristics* (Washington, D.C.: U.S. Government Printing Office, 1963), table 25, p. 296 and table 26, p. 215; U.S. Department of Interior, Bureau of Indian Affairs, "Selected Data on Indian Reservations Eligible for Designation Under Public Works and Economic Development Act" of Commerce, Bureau of the Census, 1970 Census of Population, *American Indians* (Washington, D.C.: U.S. Government Printing Office, 1973), table 13, pp. 161–163; and U.S. Department of Commerce, Bureau of the Census, 1970 Census of Population, *Education* (Washington D.C.: U.S. Government Printing Office, 1973), table 7, pp. 149–151.
Note: Data include all males and all sources of income, whether earned or unearned.

---

[22] Alan L. Sorkin, The Urban American Indian (Lexington, Mass.: Lexington Books, 1978), p. 14.

In addition, as shown on the ''Median Income'' table, from 1939 to 1969 the median income of reservation Indians averaged less than half that of whites, which rose less than that of reservation Indians during this period. By 1959, the median income of non-reservation Indians was nearly that of non-whites.[23]

The source of income for reservation Indians has changed fundamentally: in 1939, 38% came from wages, 26% from agriculture, 8% from arts and crafts, 28% was unearned. In 1964, an estimated 75% of the total income was derived from wages, with 10% from agriculture, 5% from arts and crafts, and 10% unearned.[24]

There is great variation in income among reservations. Median family income in 1979 varied from a low of $4,452 on the Muckleshoot reservation to $50,394 on the Agua Caliente reservation as shown in the table on page 12. Even within a state the variation is sizeable. In California, median income on the Santa Rosa Rancheria reservation was less than one-quarter of that on the Agua Caliente reservation; in Washington, median income on the Muckleshoot reservation was less than one-third of that on the Colville reservation.[25]

---

[23] Ibid.

[24] Sorkin, American Indians and Federal Aid, pp. 9—10.

[25] Tom Arrandale, ''American Indian Economic Development,'' Editorial Research Reports, V. 1 No. 7, Feb. 17, 1984, p. 129.

Indian Reservation Income, 1979[26]
Selected Reservations

Reservation	State	Per Capita Income	Median Family Income	Persons Below Poverty Level
Agua Caliente	Calif.	$6,409	$50,394	34.9%
Osage	Okla.	5,806	15,891	18.5
Onondaga	N.Y.	5,693	17,742	18.9
Penobscot	Maine	4,861	9,208	21.4
Colville	Wash.	4,428	12,394	32.7
Laguna Pueblo	N.M.	4,422	16,675	12.3
Red Lake	Minn.	4,106	12,465	28.9
Potawatomi	Wis.	3,799	3,523	58.9
Lummi	Wash.	3,783	15,893	24.6
Brighton Seminole	Fla.	3,769	7,279	34.4
Turtle Mountain	N.D.	3,339	10,934	40.8
Indian Township	Maine	3,260	15,556	27.8
Eastern Cherokee	N.C.	3,066	9,849	34.0
Crow	Mont.	3,011	9,773	33.1
Mississippi Choctaw	Miss.	2,988	11,054	35.2
Acoma Pueblo	N.M.	2,885	14,225	29.7
Fort Berthold	N.D.	2,730	11,045	37.5
Northern Cheyenne	Mont.	2,512	9,336	41.8
Hopi	Ariz.	2,510	8,145	50.2
Rosebud	S.D.	2,484	8,318	50.2
Navajo	Ariz., N.M., Utah	2,414	9,079	49.7
Fort Apache	Ariz.	2,309	10,129	42.2
Pine Ridge	S.D.	2,209	9,435	48.5
Fort McDermitt	Nev., Ore.	1,982	7,917	61.5
Santa Rosa Rancheria	Calif.	1,322	—	36.4
Muckleshoot	Wash.	1,094	4,452	68.8

Source: U.S. Department of Commerce, Bureau of the Census, 1980 Census

[26] Ibid.

The strikingly low level of Indians' income is associated with unemployment rates several times those of non—Indians (as shown in table on page 14). While the rate for all Indians fell 4.3% between 1940 and 1970, the rate for blacks fell 9.8%; for whites, 10.8%. The increase is chiefly a result of the riot exodus of Indians from agriculture in search of better—paid employment. Since most of them lack training and education, they are restricted to unskilled occupations with high rates of unemployment, particularly on reservations where there has been little industrialization.[27]

We must not forget that there were many pioneer organizers who, in good faith, sought to bring about laws to secure land and protection for the hapless Indians. Even though many of these laws proved to be inadequate, the losses ultimately suffered by the Indians could have been even greater. However, there have been bills and laws passed that, to this day, proved to be a long and bitter campaign for a complete overhaul of Indian affairs. One such bill was the so—called Bursum Lands Bill in 1922.

This bill proposed to establish a procedure by which white settlers could perfect title to lands which they had entered and improved or purchased in good faith (so they claimed), believing the land to be part of the public domain and open to homestead entry, or held

---

[27] Sorkin, The Urban American Indian, p. 21.

Unemployment Rates, Indian, Black, and White Males, Selected Years, 1940–1975[28]
(in percent)

Year	Indians			Blacks	Whites
	All	**Urban**	**Reservation**		
1940	32.9	—	—	18.0	14.8
1950	—	15.1	—	9.6	5.9
1958	—	—	43.5	13.8	6.1
1960	38.2	12.1	51.3	10.7	4.8
1962	—	—	43.4	10.9	4.6
1965	—	—	41.9	7.4	3.6
1967	—	—	37.3	6.0	2.7
1970	28.6	9.4	41.0	8.2	4.0
1972	—	—	40.0	10.0	4.5
1975	—	—	39.8	13.7	7.2

Sources: U.S. Department of Labor, *Manpower Report of the President,* 1973 (Washington, D.C.: U.S. Government Printing Office, 1973), p. 145; U.S. Department of Commerce, Bureau of the Census, 1940 Census of Population, *Characteristics of the Nonwhite Population by Race* (Washington, D.C.: U.S. Government Printing Office, 1943), table 25, p. 82; U.S. Department of Commerce, Bureau of the Census, 1940 Census of Population, *The Labor Force* (Washington, D.C.: U.S. Government Printing Office, 1943), table 4, p. 18; U.S. Department of Commerce, Bureau of the Census, 1950 Census of Population, *Nonwhite Population by Race* (Washington, D.C.: U.S. Government Printing Office, 1953), table 10, p. 32; U.S. Department of Commerce, Bureau of the Census, 1960 Census of Population, *Nonwhite Population by Race* (Washington, D.C.: U.S. Government Printing Office, 1963), table 33, p. 104; U.S. Department of Interior, Bureau of Indian Affairs, *Indian Unemployment Survey* (Washington, D.C.: U.S. Government Printing Office, 1963); U.S. Department of Interior, Bureau of Indian Affairs, unpublished tabulation (December 1967); U.S. Department of Interior, Bureau of Indian Affairs, "Estimates of Resident Indian Population and Labor Force Status, by State and Reservation, March 1972" (Washington, D.C.: U.S. Department of Interior, 1973), mimeographed; and U.S. Department of Interior, Bureau of Indian Affairs, "Estimates of Resident Indian Population and Labor Force Status, by State and Reservation, April 1975" (Washington, D.C.: U.S. Department of Interior, 1975), mimeographed.

Note: Data for Indians in all years and blacks and whites in 1940 include those 14 years old and over; all other data include males 16 years old and over.

---

[28] *Ibid.*

in private ownership and subject to conveyance. In reality, the lands lay inside the boundaries of grants conveyed by Spain to the Pueblo Indians in New Mexico. The proposed legislation placed upon the Indians the burden of proving their lawful ownership, thus reversing the established legal procedure which requires a person in adverse possession to prove ownership. Some 3,000 white squatters or families, representing perhaps 12,000 persons, and many thousands of acres were involved.[29]

The campaign of public education which brought about the defeat of the original Bursum proposal and the eventual passage of an equitable Pueblo Lands Act also called forth new citizens' groups, two of which are still active in Indian Affairs. The New Mexico Association, now the Southwestern Association on Indian Affairs, was formed in 1922, and the American Indian Defense League followed soon after. The latter organization experienced several structural changes. One group moved its base of operations eastward to become the Eastern Association on Indian Affairs, and later changed its name to the National Association on Indian Affairs, and still later (1936) formed a new amalgamation with the parent Indian Defense League. The resulting organization is the Association on

---

[29] Robert C. Euler and Henry F. Dobyns, ''Ethnic Group Land Rights in the Modern State,'' Human Organization, 3 (1961–62), p. 210.

American Indian Affairs of today—sometimes referred to in hostile government reports as . . . that eastern organization for Indians.[30]

Another law of inadequacy was the law of May 28, 1830. In connection with a series of treaties, it set apart for the Indians the country lying west of Missouri and Arkansas, and provided for the removal there of numerous tribes, not only from the reservations east of the Mississippi but also from the states and organized territories west of that river. Between 1840 and 1850, the map showed an ''Indian Territory,'' stretching from the Red River to the Platte, while the Sioux and other tribes retained, almost unnoticed, the country further north. In a few years, however, conditions demanded the organization of the northern portions of this great tract.[31]

We must realize that the loss of land and economic status of the American Indian is closely related to his educational attainment. The median level of schooling of the Indian male in 1960 was less than the 1940 level of white males (as shown in the table on page 17). Although the median level of Indians increased by more than four years

---

[30] Ibid., p. 210.

[31] Roy Gittinger, ''The Separation of Nebraska and Kansas from the Indian Territory,'' Mississippi Valley Historical Review, 3 (March 1914—20), p. 442.

Percent Distribution of Indian, Black, and White Males by Years of School Completed, 1940, 1960, and 1970[32]

Years of School Completed	Indian				
				1970	
	1940	1960	Total	Urban	Rural
0	23.9	9.6	7.7	2.7	12.3
1–4	20.1	12.6	7.7	5.2	10.1
5–8	38.7	37.8	28.0	23.8	31.8
9–11	9.6	22.8	23.3	24.8	21.9
12	4.9	11.6	22.0	26.9	17.6
13–15	2.0	4.0	7.5	10.8	4.5
16 or more	0.7	1.6	3.8	5.9	1.8
Median	5.5	8.4	9.8	11.2	8.7

Years of School Completed	Black			White		
	1940	1960	1970	1940	1960	1970
0	8.1	5.0	2.2	1.2	0.9	0.7
1–4	33.4	17.7	10.1	5.5	3.8	2.3
5–8	41.2	36.2	27.4	42.2	28.9	19.9
9–11	9.9	22.7	25.1	20.0	20.2	20.5
12	4.6	12.1	23.2	18.4	24.8	31.5
13–15	1.8	4.0	6.9	7.0	9.8	10.6
16 or more	1.1	2.2	5.2	5.8	11.6	14.5
Median	5.3	8.3	10.2	8.7	12.2	12.3

Sources: U.S. Department of Commerce, Bureau of the Census, 1940 Census of Population, *Characteristics of the Nonwhite Population by Race* (Washington, D.C.: U.S. Government Printing Office, 1943), table 24, p. 80; U.S. Department of Commerce, Bureau of the Census, 1940 Census of Population, *Educational Attainment by Economic Characteristics and Marital Status* (Washington, D.C.: U.S. Government Printing Office, 1943), table 17, p. 75 and table 18, p. 82; U.S. Department of Commerce, Bureau of the Census, 1960 Census of Population, *Nonwhite Population by Race* (Washington, D.C.: U.S. Government Printing Office, 1963), table 9, p. 9 and table 10, p. 12; U.S. Department of Commerce, Bureau of the Census, 1960 Census of Population, *Educational Attainment* (Washington, D.C.: U.S. Government Printing Office, 1963), table 1, p. 1; U.S. Department of Commerce, Bureau of the Census, 1970 Census of Population, *American Indians* (Washington, D.C.: U.S. Government Printing Office, 1973), table 5, pp. 36–39; and U.S. Department of Commerce, Bureau of the Census, 1970 Census of Population, *Educational Attainment* (Washington, D.C.: U.S. Government Printing Office, 1973), table 5, pp. 104 and 106.

---

[32] Sorkin, *The Urban American Indian*, p. 19.

from 1940 to 1970, in 1970 the percentage of Indians attending college was only about one–third that of white males, and the percentage of Indians with no schooling or fewer than five years was almost double that of all males. Between 1940 and 1970, the median educational attainment of Indians and blacks was about the same, while two to three times as many Indians as blacks had no formal education.[33]

The early history of the United States and the part the American Indian played reveals through analysis that the government took the land from the American Indians and impoverished them. The beginning of impoverishment started with the first kidnapping of Indians into slavery, followed by mass murder, destruction of villages, and continuous forceful movement of Indians. The Indians sought revenge, but many died in vain. They trusted in the white man's peace treaties with them, but promises were continuously broken down through the years up to this present date.

A quotation by Heinmot Tooyalaket (Chief Joseph) of the Nez Perces, explicitly expresses how they feel about this land: ''The earth was created by the assistance of the sun, and it should be left as it was. . . . The country was made without lines of demarcation, and it is no man's business to divide it. . . . I see the whites all over the country gaining wealth, and see their desire

---

[33] Ibid.

to give us lands which are worthless. . . . The earth and myself are of one mind. The measure of the land and the measure of our bodies are the same. Say to us if you can say it, that you were sent by the Creative Power to talk to us. Perhaps you think the Creator sent you here to dispose of us as you see fit. If I thought you were sent by the Creator I might be induced to think you had a right to dispose of me. Do not misunderstand me, but understand me fully with reference to my affection for the land. I never said the land was mine to do with it as I chose. The one who has the right to dispose of it is the one who has created it. I claim a right to live on my land, and accord you the privilege to live on yours.''[34]

---

[34] Brown, p. 300.

BIBLIOGRAPHY

Arrandale, Tom. ''American Indian Economic Development.'' Editorial Research Reports, Vol. 1, no. 7 (Feb. 17, 1984):127–144.

Brown, Dee. Bury My Heart at Wounded Knee. New York: Holt, Rinehart and Winston, 1970.

Euler, Robert C., and Henry F. Dobyns. ''Ethnic Group Land Rights in the Modern State.'' Human Organization. 3 (1961–62): 210.

Gittinger, Roy. ''The Separation of Nebraska and Kansas from the Indian Territory.'' Mississippi Valley Historical Review. 3 (March 1914–20): 442.

Sorkin, Alan L. American Indians and Federal Aid. Washington, D.C.: The Brookings Institution, 1971.

——. The Urban American Indian. Lexington, Mass.: D.C. Heath and Co., 1978.

C—Transitional Words and Phrases

1. *Addition:* one, another, similarly, moreover, furthermore, in addition, too, again, equally important, next, finally, first, second (etc.), besides, likewise, in the same way.

2. *Contrast:* yet, however, still, nevertheless, on the one hand / on the other hand, on the contrary, notwithstanding, for all that, by contrast, at the same time, although, while, a different view, in spite of, despite.

3. *Comparison:* similarly, likewise, in like manner, both, each, in the same way.

4. *Conclusion:* therefore, thus, then, consequently, as a consequence, as a result, accordingly, finally, for this (these) reason(s), on that account, because of, under these conditions, since.

5. *Explanation:* for example, to illustrate, by way of illustration, to be specific, specifically, in particular, thus, for instance, in other words.

6. *Concession:* naturally, granted, of course, to be sure, although, despite, in spite of, notwithstanding, for all, while.

7. *Time:* when, immediately, upon, since, first, earlier, meanwhile, at the same time, in the meantime, soon afterward, subsequently, later.

8. *Summation, Repetition, Intensification:* to sum up, in brief, in short, in fact, indeed, in other words.

D—Self-Evaluation Guide

Form

1. Will your paper be ready on time? Many instructors lower the grades on late papers.

2. Is your paper the correct length? Most students write papers that are too short rather than too long.

3. Footnotes—(a) Do they follow the correct form?

   (b) Are they placed properly?

4. Bibliography—(a) Have you used enough sources?

   (b) Have you followed the correct form?

5. Is your paper neatly typed with few errors and proper margins?

6. Have you met *all* of the specifications given by this book or your instructor?

Style

1. Is your paper well organized? Does each part relate to the whole? Does the development of your ideas follow a logical order?

2. Is your grammar, spelling, and punctuation correct?

3. Does your paper flow smoothly? Have you used transitional words and sentences to link the different parts of the paper?

4. Have you used synonyms to avoid too much repetition in your vocabulary?

5. Are your sentences clearly constructed—not too short or choppy, not too long or hard to follow?

Content

1. Are your topic and thesis relevant to the assignment you were given? Is your thesis important enough to write about?

2. Does your introduction really "introduce" your paper? Do you have a good opening sentence? Do you state your thesis so that the reader knows what your paper is about?

3. Does each succeeding paragraph amplify at least one main idea?

4. Have you used recognized, up-to-date sources? Have you used enough sources to substantiate your thesis? Have you used a variety of sources—books, periodicals, newspapers, interviews, etc.?

5. Does your conclusion summarize and restate your thesis in a final way, using the results of your research?

Final Evaluation

Can you grade your own paper in each of the above areas?

Form

Style

Content

A—excellent, outstanding work

B—very good

C—fair

D—poor

F—does not meet acceptable standards

NOTES

NOTES

NOTES

NOTES

BOOKS FOR COLLEGE-BOUND STUDENTS

COLLEGE ENTRANCE

ACT: American College Testing Program
ACT Cram Course
ACT English Workbook
ACT Math Workbook
ACT SuperCourse
AP American History
AP Biology
AP Chemistry
AP Computer Science
AP English Composition and Literature
AP European History
AP Mathematics
College Board Achievement Test
  in Mathematics: Level I
College Board Achievement Test
  in Mathematics: Level II
College Board Achievement Test in Spanish
College Board Achievement Tests SuperCourse
Nursing School Entrance Examinations
PCAT: Pharmacy College Admissions Test
Preparation for the SAT: Scholastic Assessment Test
SAT Cram Course
SAT Math Workbook
SAT SuperCourse
SAT Verbal Workbook
SAT-II Writing
TOEFL: Test of English as a Foreign Language
TOEFL Grammar Workbook
TOEFL Reading and Vocabulary Workbook
TOEFL Skills for Top Scores
TOEFL SuperCourse

COLLEGE GUIDES

The American Film Institute Guide to College Courses
  in Film and Television
College Applications and Essays

College Financial Aid
College Survival
Lovejoy's College Guide
The Performing Arts Major's College Guide
The Right College
The Transfer Student's Guide

STUDY AIDS

Associated Press Guide to News Writing
Consumer and Business Mathematics
College Time Tracker
Essential English Composition for College-Bound
  Students
Essential Math for College-Bound Students
Essential Vocabulary for College-Bound
  Students
High School Time Tracker
How to Develop and Write a Research Paper
How to Read and Interpret Poetry
How to Read and Write about Drama
How to Read and Write about Fiction
How to Solve Algebra Word Problems
How to Write Book Reports
How to Write Poetry
How to Write Short Stories
How to Write Themes and Essays
How to Write a Thesis
1001 Ideas for Science Projects
Reading Lists for College-Bound Students
10,000 Ideas for Term Papers, Projects, Reports,
  and Speeches
Triple Your Reading Speed
Webster's New World™ Power Vocabulary
Webster's New World™ Student Writing
  Handbook

AVAILABLE AT BOOKSTORES EVERYWHERE

PRENTICE HALL

BOOKS FOR GRADUATE SCHOOL AND BEYOND

ARCO'S SUPERCOURSES

GMAT SuperCourse
GRE SuperCourse
LSAT SuperCourse
MCAT SuperCourse
TOEFL SuperCourse

TOEFL

TOEFL: Test of English as a Foreign Language
TOEFL Grammar Workbook
TOEFL Reading and Vocabulary Workbook
TOEFL Skills for Top Scores

ARCO'S CRAM COURSES

GMAT Cram Course
GRE Cram Course
LSAT Cram Course

TEACHER CERTIFICATION

CBEST: California Educational Basic Skills Test
NTE: National Teacher Examinations
PPST: Pre-Professional Skills Tests
Teacher Certification Tests

HEALTH PROFESSIONS

Allied Health Professions
Nursing School Entrance Examinations
PCAT: Pharmacy College Admission Test

GRADUATE SCHOOL GUIDES

The Best Law Schools
Getting into Law School: Strategies for the 90's
Getting into Medical School: Strategies for the 90's
The Grad Student's Guide to Getting Published

GRADUATE & PROFESSIONAL SCHOOL ENTRANCE

GMAT: Graduate Management Admission Test
GRE: Graduate Record Examination
GRE • GMAT Math Review
Graduate Record Examination in Computer Science
Graduate Record Examination in Engineering
Graduate Record Examination in Psychology
GRE • LSAT Logic Workbook
LSAT: Law School Admission Test
MAT: Miller Analogies Test
MCAT Sample Exams

AVAILABLE AT BOOKSTORES EVERYWHERE
PRENTICE HALL